A Duck Ca

By Liza Charlesworth

ISBN: 978-1-339-02674-9

Art Director: Tannaz Fassihi; Designer: Tanya Chernyak
Photos © Getty Images and Shutterstock.com.
Copyright © Liza Charlesworth. All rights reserved. Published by Scholastic Inc.

3 4 5 6 7 8 9 10   68   32 31 30 29 28 27 26 25 24

Printed in Jiaxing, China. First printing, August 2023.

SCHOLASTIC

See the ducks!
They quack, quack, quack!
They will not quit.

A duck can be tan
or white or black.

Ducks rest on rocks.

Hop! Ducks dip in ponds.

Is a duck quick? Yes!
It can kick its legs fast.

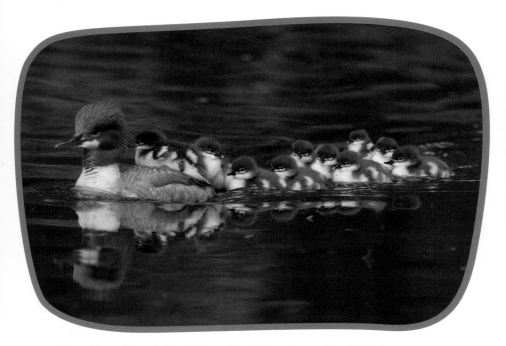

1, 2, 3, 4, 5, 6, 7, 8, 9, 10!
A mom duck can swim
with ten tots.

Quack, quack, quack!
A lot of ducks is a flock.

Flap, flap, flap!
A flock can flap off.
Will the ducks be back?